T0121520

How to Develop a

# PROPHETIC
# CULTURE

## JOHN HARKE

WESTBOW
PRESS®
A DIVISION OF THOMAS NELSON
& ZONDERVAN

Copyright © 2017 John Harke.

All rights reserved. No part of this book may be used or reproduced by any means, graphic, electronic, or mechanical, including photocopying, recording, taping or by any information storage retrieval system without the written permission of the author except in the case of brief quotations embodied in critical articles and reviews.

Scripture taken from the New King James Version®. Copyright © 1982 by Thomas Nelson. Used by permission. All rights reserved.

Scripture quotations marked (NIV) are taken from the Holy Bible, New International Version®, NIV®. Copyright © 1973, 1978, 1984, 2011 by Biblica, Inc.™ Used by permission of Zondervan. All rights reserved worldwide. www.zondervan.com The "NIV" and "New International Version" are trademarks registered in the United States Patent and Trademark Office by Biblica, Inc.™

Scripture quotations taken from the Amplified® Bible (AMP), Copyright © 2015 by The Lockman Foundation Used by permission. www.Lockman.org

Scripture quoted by permission. Quotations designated (NET) are from The NET Bible® Copyright © 2005 by Biblical Studies Press, L.L.C. www.bible.org All rights reserved.

WestBow Press books may be ordered through booksellers or by contacting:

WestBow Press
A Division of Thomas Nelson & Zondervan
1663 Liberty Drive
Bloomington, IN 47403
www.westbowpress.com
1 (866) 928-1240

Because of the dynamic nature of the Internet, any web addresses or links contained in this book may have changed since publication and may no longer be valid. The views expressed in this work are solely those of the author and do not necessarily reflect the views of the publisher, and the publisher hereby disclaims any responsibility for them.

Any people depicted in stock imagery provided by Thinkstock are models, and such images are being used for illustrative purposes only.
Certain stock imagery © Thinkstock.

ISBN: 978-1-9736-0198-2 (sc)
ISBN: 978-1-9736-0197-5 (e)

Library of Congress Control Number: 2017914096

Print information available on the last page.

WestBow Press rev. date: 09/27/2017

# CHAPTER ONE

# BURNING WITH PROPHETIC PASSION

Numbers 11:26-29 (*NKJV*)
*But two men had remained in the camp: the name of one was Eldad, and the name of the other Medad. And the Spirit rested upon them. Now they were among those listed, but who had not gone out to the tabernacle; yet they prophesied in the camp. ²⁷ And a young man ran and told Moses, and said, "Eldad and Medad are prophesying in the camp." ²⁸ So Joshua the son of Nun, Moses' assistant, one of his choice men, answered and said, "Moses my lord, forbid them!" ²⁹ Then Moses said to him, "Are you zealous for my sake? Oh, that all the LORD's people were prophets and that the LORD would put His Spirit upon them!"*

When I read these verses it strikes at my heart. I'm sure Moses felt the same, when Joshua asked him to stop Medad and Eldad from prophesying. We see here the Lord's desire for a prophetic culture -- people with inspiration and power upon their lives. A prophetic culture is one that is hearing God and burning to bless the broken and the weak, speaking the word of God into seemingly hopeless situations.

*Training up a prophetic culture*

There are three specifics in this passage that the Holy Spirit wants us to receive: impartation, instruction and activation. Impartation comes through an investment of our time, energy and resources. Many leaders would love to have a powerful anointing and great ministry, but are they willing to make the investment? A prophetic framework endorses what the Lord is resting upon. But on this occasion, Joshua was operating from an incorrect framework that actually forbid the flow of the Holy Spirit.

Prophecy is not what divides the camp – we divide the camp when we smother what the Spirit of God is doing. It isn't the flow of the Holy Spirit that divides the camp. It is jealousy that divides the camp. In this situation, Joshua saw what Medad and Eldad were doing and he became critical instead of staying under the anointing.

Are we going to forfeit the anointing because we don't like what the Lord is doing with someone else? We have to choose to put aside all our judgments, thoughts and preferences or we will have the tendency to focus upon minor details. In this instance, Joshua was not operating in the anointing. He did not necessarily forfeit his own anointing, but he did forfeit his ability to pass it on. Beloved, our destinies are connected to moments of impartation. The impartation we receive is determined by whoever or whatever we choose to stand before.

We must guard ourselves against neutrality. Being neutral can become a major hindrance to receiving the fullness of God's power upon our lives. Think of it like this: when a vehicle is in neutral, it isn't operating upon the power that's inside it. I believe that when the church yearns for the spirit of prophecy, this yearning will start her spiritual engine and initiate the momentum for awakening and revival. However, if the church remains in neutral, it will be moved by the cultural gravity surrounding it. We cannot afford to be neutral or we will never move forward. Staying in neutral will prevent us from continually flowing in the prophetic. Neutrality causes the Spirit of God to leave, because we become disengaged, instead of cultivating a heart that burns for God. How can we prevent neutrality? Neutrality can be rooted out by cultivating a life that is deeply in love with God and passionately concerned for broken humanity.

Moses' reply to Joshua addresses a lack of understanding of the Kingdom of God. When our heart falls into error like Joshua, it can potentially cause us to become cynical. But when we receive a revelation of the Kingdom of God, it replaces our doubt with a heart that is eternally hopeful. Every aspiring leader needs to be mindful of the potential of becoming sarcastic. When a leader is not experiencing God's fullness, cynicism can become a normal pattern of thinking. Such was the case with Joshua. But as we spend time with the Lord, He reveals who we really are and produces in us an eager expectation of effectiveness. We begin to gain a vision for the Lord's people, even those who are outside our own camp. It's important to take a generation into a prophetic atmosphere, because without the prophetic ministry there is no inspiration. The Lord told Moses to call the elders so He could put His Spirit upon them (Numbers 11:25, *NIV*)

and His plan for His people has not changed. The prophetic word moves all of us to be completely His because of the promise attached to it. Part of our maturing process is learning to hear the voice of God. This happens when leaders in the church impart, instruct and activate those they are leading. We must know that nothing comes into being without a prophetic vision. Numbers 11 illustrates God's vision for Israel. His will was that the entire nation become a company of prophets. He wanted them to carry the presence and power of God wherever they went, through proclamations and power demonstrations. What a privileged position and influence they were entrusted with! We too have been given these promises. I believe that the greatest impartation of the Spirit of God is being released upon the earth in this generation, to activate the people of God and to release the Kingdom of Heaven on the earth.

## *Stirred up*

Haggai 1:14 (*NIV*)
*So the Lord stirred up the spirit of Zerubbabel the son of Shealtiel, governor of Judah, and the spirit of Joshua the son of Jehozadak, the high priest, and the spirit of all the remnant of the people; and they came and worked on the house of the Lord of hosts, their God*

The Lord stirred up Zerubbabel through the prophetic word. In other words the Lord's leadership along with the people were stirred up by the Prophet's words. How do we maintain a heart that is moved for the Lord? When our heart meditates upon the high moral qualities of God, it cannot help but be stirred. "It is not good that man should be alone ... " (Gen. 2:18, *NKJV*). In the time of the prophet Haggai, it wasn't the prophetic word that was God's goal. It was the completion of the Temple that was God's goal. The Lord always desires completion. It was the beauty of the prophet's words that stirred the people's hearts. As in Psalm 45:1, the thing that stirred the psalmist's heart was that his thought life was set upon a noble theme. So his thoughts and words were consistent with what he prayed for. Also we are stirred by the voice of God saying, "Let Me in". One primary thing that keeps a man's heart stirred is consistent times of worship before the Lord. Without those times of worship, the heart disconnects from God.

What keeps the heart stirred?

1 -- A prophetic word (1 Tim 4:14, *NKJV*)
2 -- Meaningful relationships
3 -- Personal worship (2 Sam 12:20, *NKJV*)
4 -- Thoughts and words that are consistent with what we're praying for
5 -- Don't stop dreaming. (Ps 126:1, *NKJV*)

When these truths are resonating in us, a generation of powerful preachers will arise. We will be activated and instructed by spiritual fathers who yearn to impart what the Lord has given them. These fathers will impart to others without a hint of insecurity. They will rejoice when their spiritual sons and daughters are being used in the camp. And since these sons and daughters have been trained by impartation and not just by academia, they will burn with humility and passion.

Beloved, I believe that there is still an anointing that lies dormant because very few believers have a deep desire to possess the mantle of a prophet. But when a person touches the anointing, he comes alive. Therefore, this generation cannot afford to be disinterested in the prophetic impartation that the Lord has for them.

Read Numbers 11:16-30, *NIV*

Questions to ask:

* Why was the Lord so concerned about putting Moses' anointing upon the elders?
* Why did the elders prophesy and then stop? (Numbers 11:25, *NIV*)

* Why did Joshua want Moses to forbid Medad and Eldad to prophesy?
* Why did Moses want all the Lord's people to be prophets?
* How do we keep from being cynical and stay stirred up in our spirit?
* What can we do to posture ourselves for impartation, instruction and activation in the prophetic ministry?

Apprehending the truth

After we learn how to keep our hearts stirred, what is the next step? It is crucial that we surround ourselves with good examples. There are many in the body of Christ and those in history who have walked in power and influence. Through both their successes and mistakes we can receive impartation. Also we must understand that Jesus' desire is to make us great and the process by which we are made great is by serving (Mark 10:42-43, *NIV*). When we have a heart that is willing to serve others, we position ourselves to receive the greatest impartation, which is knowing Him intimately. Out of this intimate relationship with Him we become voices that empower, equip and encourage a generation.

# CHAPTER TWO

# KEEPING OUR PROPHETIC EDGE

Genesis 19:14, *NIV*

*"So Lot went out and spoke to his sons-in-law, who were pledged to marry[a] his daughters. He said, "Hurry and get out of this place, because the Lord is about to destroy the city!" But his sons-in-law thought he was joking."*

We see that people who are unchanged severely limit the spirit of prophecy from flowing in their lives and they only produce conflict. Lot's example is one that we need to reflect upon, if we are going to mature in the prophetic ministry (Genesis 13:7- 11, *NKJV*). Sadly Lot separated not only from his uncle, but from his spiritual father. He made a careless disconnection from Abraham, not taking into consideration God's hand on Abraham. There was conflict between those in Lot's household and Moses' household, but we also see here a demonstration of Lot's independent spirit. This independence continued throughout Lot's life, despite a visitation from two heavenly messengers and the counsel of an uncle who was a prophet and the father of nations. All of us who yearn to keep ourselves spirituality alert, must put humility before our own independence or we have the potential to miss God's instruction. Learning that lesson requires both insight and connecting with our spiritual fathers, even in conflict.

We must understand that friction is always a part of growth. Without it we never learn community. When there is conflict in the church, we think it's much easier to simply remove ourselves in order to find our way to wholeness. That certainly was Lot's answer. I believe the Word is showing us that Lot could have taken a different route, which would not have lead him into Sodom and Gomorrah. It would have lead him on a much different path, one completely away from evil. We must remember that no matter how attractive something may be to our flesh, it is never worth sacrificing our anointing.

Genesis 13:7-1, *NKJV*
*And there was strife between the herdsmen of Abram's livestock and the herdsmen of Lot's livestock. The Canaanites and the Perizzites then dwelt in the land. So Abram said to Lot, "Please let there be no strife between you and me, and between my herdsmen and your herdsmen; for we are brethren. Is not the whole land before you? Please separate from me. If you take the left, then I will go to the right; or, if you go to the right, then I will go to the left." And Lot lifted his eyes and saw all the plain of Jordan, that it was well watered everywhere (before the Lord destroyed Sodom and Gomorrah) like the garden of the Lord, like the land of Egypt as you go toward Zoar. Then Lot chose for himself all the plain of Jordan, and Lot journeyed east. And they separated from each other.*

This passage is a parable of how our prophetic vision can get blurred. If we as the church are going to keep our prophetic edge, we must understand that strife indicates a deep internal defect which affects our most important relationships. Strife can be like an aggressive cancer spreading through the body. When those who are outside the family of God see the church fighting internally, strife hinders our ability to influence the culture that so desperately needs to hear a word from the Lord. Therefore we need to see strife as an enemy. At its core, strife is a struggle for superiority.

Lot's uncle Abraham truly wanted to hear the voice of God in the midst of inner turmoil. And hearing in this way requires great humility and patience. Abraham shows the heart of a true spiritual father who is deeply concerned about drawing the family into a place of wholeness. When strife exists, it displays how unhealthy the heart is and clogs our ability to discern revelation. So when we read the word or pray there is no prophetic anointing. In order to maintain this sharpness in the prophetic it takes a heart that will honor and prefer those who we are in disagreement with. And like Abraham it takes having love for those who don't see things the way we do.

Other people need to witness a prophetic generation that has a healthy heart. When the heart is in good condition there isn't any room for a combative attitude. The attitude, actions and intercession of those with healthy hearts transform those around them who are emotionally weak. To deal with the conflict, Abraham looks for a way to bring peace to the situation between Lot's herdsmen and his own. This is the sign of a genuine prophetic heart. So it's no surprise that the Lord continued to speak clearly to Abraham throughout his life. Lot had his eye upon what benefited him at the moment – Abraham had his eye upon God. Abraham knew that even if he chose the wilderness, it was the place where God's voice could be heard -- the place of transformation and blessing. Let's take this truth to heart: attitude is the mirror of our thought life. But let's look at the Lord's attitude toward us, because when the Lord speaks through the prophetic ministry He is showing us the mirror of His thoughts toward His people.

Genesis 14:14, *NKJV*
*Now when Abram heard that his brother was taken captive, he armed his three hundred and eighteen trained servants who were born in his own house, and went in pursuit as far as Dan.*

Shortly after the separation with Abraham, Lot finds himself in captivity. Notice how Abraham addressed Lot, not as a nephew or a person who caused strife, but as a brother. With that heart, of course God saw Abraham as a father and a prophet. I believe this is how we in the church also have to respond. This man of God used his own resources to rescue the one who had brought strife and separated from him! Abraham understood his moral obligation to Lot even when Lot chose to break away from him. One fact we see in this beautiful story is that we will not rescue someone unless we care about their welfare. Yet even after the miraculous deliverance that Abraham brought to his nephew, Lot still chose to move closer to Sodom and Gomorrah. As the angels of the Lord approach the city, we find Lot at the city gate.

Genesis 19:1, *NKJV*
*Now the two angels came to Sodom in the evening, and Lot was sitting in the gate of Sodom. When Lot saw them, he rose to meet them, and he bowed himself with his face toward the ground.*

How did Lot get a position at the city gate? I believe that his first mistake was moving away from covenant with Abraham and into covenant with Sodom and Gomorrah. When we as the Lord's people make wrong covenants with others outside, we diminish the prophetic spirit that could potentially rest upon us. We experience mental confusion and injure our ability to hear the voice of the Lord correctly. The voice of the Lord can be tainted by our wrong judgements. So for Lot to be seated where he was, he had to be assimilated into the culture of Sodom. We understand that he held some governmental position because decisions were made at the city gates. But we should never use political influence to bring change to society. I'm not saying we shouldn't vote or be a part of the political process. But our influence should come through the anointing of God and not through a political agenda. This is what happened to Lot when he turned toward politics and away from the prophetic.

We must look clearly at church history and recognize that spirit and the damage it has done to the church. Of course government is vital, for without it we promote anarchy. I'm sure Lot thought he could influence Sodom and Gomorrah at first, but instead he slowly lost his vision and commitment to the Lord.

2 Peter 2:8, *NKJV*
*(for that righteous man, dwelling among them, tormented his righteous soul from day to day by seeing and hearing their lawless deeds)*

If you and I are going to gain influence in this broken world, we must stay in covenant relationally and stay away from anything that would prevent us from hearing His voice. Let's look again at the concept of keeping our prophetic edge.

Genesis 19:14, *NKJV*
*So Lot went out and spoke to his sons-in-law, who had married his daughters, and said, "Get up, get out of this place; for the Lord will destroy this city!" But to his sons-in-law he seemed to be joking.*

These future in-laws believed that Lot was joking and began to mock the word of warning from the Lord. They did not take Lot's words seriously and they wrongfully thought that Lot was ridiculing their lifestyle. Their indifference shows how morally insensitive they had become. A prophetic voice of grace had been sent to them through Lot. So why didn't they take into consideration what he said? I'm certain of this, as a result of living with the sin of Sodom and Gomorrah, Lot had lost his prophetic edge. He no longer had the ability to convince or convict his family of the coming judgment. This revelation burns in my spirit. The cry to convince a world of the goodness of God – not to destroy those who are caught in the web of darkness, but to rescue them. Lot had become like everyone else and therefore had no power to convict them of their error. There is

11

coming upon the church a fresh anointing to convince others of the Lord's heart! As we the people of God live like the One we love, our ability to persuade nations to pursue the presence of God and His righteous decrees will increase.

Read Genesis 19:1-29, *NKJV*

Questions to ask

* Why is covenant relationship so important in developing a prophetic culture?
* Do you believe that internal strife limits our ability to discern the Lord's voice?
* Why did Lot go from being in the plains of Sodom and Gomorrah to being involved in the city?
* God asked Lot if he had any other family. What does this tell us about His heart?
* Is there something in my own heart that is inhibiting God's voice from speaking through me?
* What can I do to keep that prophetic edge to convince the world of Jesus's goodness?

Apprehending the truth

There is so much to ponder through the story of Lot's life -- the insanity of people's choices and the mercy of Heaven that rescues them from that insanity. A prophet prays and God moves, when all others want to do is sin. The prophet reclaims what should have never left covenant in the first place. It is so astonishing that God takes our vocal cords and puts prophecy upon them. Let's never take that gift for granted by patterning our lives after things that are unlike Him.

## CHAPTER THREE

# ALERT TO HIS VOICE

Isaiah 50:4, *NIV*
*The Sovereign Lord has given me a well-instructed tongue, to know the word that sustains the weary. He wakens me morning by morning, wakens my ear to listen like one being instructed.*

Can you imagine writing this about yourself: "my tongue is well instructed"? When I read this passage, I can't help but ask how Isaiah's tongue became well instructed. I'm fascinated by the language that the prophet uses. He touches on both practical application and revelation.

The prophetic gift unveils a portion of the abundance that the Lord has stored up for us. Teaching us all what it means to be alert to the Lord's voice. Especially since there are still many in church culture who are tone deaf to the prophetic ministry. The prophet's tongue was *touched* to purge it from sinful speech. But it was also *taught* to decree what the Lord was saying without the fear of man. In this chapter we will focus upon this key verse for the prophetic ministry.

*"The Sovereign Lord has given me"*

Isaiah begins to recognize that what God has given him is the best reward. This truth needs to be preached in all circles within the church. Many people find rewards in circumstances, in ministry success, or in popularity. These rewards are a tremendous blessing, but they have the potential to cause us to perform instead of prophesying the heart of God. People have a tendency to look for validation through the size of their platform rather than the size of their love for God. Then if a certain goal is not reached or if it is delayed, they tire of it and find themselves burned out or offended. On the other hand, when our goal is simply to know Him, we lose our need for public recognition. Then, no matter how gifted we become, we refuse to push ourselves to the center of the stage. We no longer have the desire to become a public figure. The prophet is preaching this verse to bring us out of the septic tank of what we think makes us happy, and into a place of reformation where holiness and prophecy fills the church once again. When this is realized, there burns within us a deep sense of urgency. Knowing this truth then sharpens our prophetic ear and fills our voices with what needs to be said in our generation.

Authenticity in the prophetic ministry is absolutely vital. It is never to promote the gift or the individual, it is to show the way of righteousness in behavior and message. Sometimes we are misunderstood and spoken about negatively, but what God has given us we never have to validate by society.

As Isaiah acknowledged what the Lord had given him, he opened the door for an increase of prophetic vision. Gratitude and the prophetic work hand in hand. As we thank Him for speaking and imparting revelation to us, it causes the Lord's heart to smile with favor upon us. Then His presence fills us with great grace to release the message He gave us, without the fear of man. What He has given is the seed to birth a prophetic culture that pursues heartfelt worship and the spirit of prophecy. This is the culture of the end time church as its prophets decree His word to the world.

*"a well-instructed tongue" (Isaiah 50:4, NIV)*

The spirit of prophecy had been poured upon Isaiah's lips and his experience at the throne of God became the anchor of his heart. This gave the prophet not only a tongue that had been made clean, but a tongue full of counsel for God's people. Isaiah's voice became a plumb line that would set things straight. You see, the prophetic ministry isn't limited to simply predicting the future. The prophetic ministry is what the Holy Spirit uses to educate His church. Isaiah is remembering when he stood before the presence of God and one of the seraphim touched his lips. That encounter transformed his preaching and -- even more importantly -- transformed his heart. He became a man of feeling and passion. He felt for both the rich and the poor, the addict and those that challenged him. He refused to make distinctions because of economic status; he served because he loved both God and people. He prophesied because the One who gave him the message had fully captured his heart. His soul had been thoroughly penetrated by the supernatural character of God. That is why the prophet's eye wasn't focused toward the enemy's activity, but instead was focused around the throne of God.

In order to have the same tongue that Isaiah had we must become fully fascinated with the Lord's presence and beauty as Isaiah was. When that happens to a church culture we become voices that shake nations and break false foundations. Through our prophetic proclamations and decrees we will unleash God's will upon the earth. And by wisdom we speak words that will nurture peace and unity, destroying the enemy's devices. How privileged we are to have been taught by the Holy Spirit, how glorious to hear His instructions toward men and women! In these days, unlike any time in history, the Spirit of God is putting His word upon a generation of men and women. The Lord is raising up many people who will be skilled in their speech to impart the knowledge of God. It's time for the church to position themselves to receive what God is pouring out. We must respond to the challenge so we can be instrumental in instructing a culture that is not in tune with Heaven.

*"to know the word that sustains the weary." (Isaiah 50:4, NIV)*

Wisdom carries the right words to lift up those who are exhausted. Prophecy opens the understanding of God's will. Isaiah in this passage is giving us a remedy for the weary. We need to cry out for a word that sustains the people of God. The prophet is intensely conscious when the Lord's heart has been crushed by hard circumstances in the lives of His people. Their lives have become shaped by negative events instead of being shaped by the thoughts of God. Isaiah's sermon to the nation of Israel is a call to feed upon the Lord's compassion and faithfulness. The oracles that the Lord gives the prophet burn in their souls. With reverence they embrace correction. Knowing that by humbly bowing down in respect toward the Lord's presence, the reward will be having the Lord pour His heart and mind toward them. Yet they sense the need for more men and women to experience a revisitation.

The Lord has raised the prophet up because His people have gotten their priorities out of order. With passion the prophet instills the thirst to discover the ways of God. With an inner awareness of the presence of God, Isaiah feels the love God has for His people. Isaiah's heart has been won by what he has heard and what he has seen. In this verse we see that the prophet has a deep yearning to sustain a people who are weighed down by fear and anxiety. Within the next decade I believe that church structures will go through tremendous transformation, energizing an entire section of the body of Christ. The word of the Lord will once again be preached with power and pulpits across the nations will be lit on fire. The freshness of the presence of Jesus and a community of worshipping believers will fall under the power of God, as God proclaims His goodness over them. Like no other time in our lives, we must lay everything before the presence of God. We should ask for the same sustaining word that Isaiah received. Depression and weariness have become an epidemic across the nation and there is an urgent need not just for more reporters but more prophets. Prophets who carry upon them not just information but who carry the language of God.

*"He wakens me morning by morning" (Isaiah 50:4, NIV)*

The prophet is never idle. He is awakened each day to anticipate what the Lord will speak to him. He gazes every morning with expectation upon the beauty and mercy of God. He can't wait for the morning! "What will the Lord tell me? For I know it will be good." In this verse Isaiah is telling us Who has his first thoughts. You see, when the Lord awakens His servants, it is to tell them how He feels and how He thinks. He shares what moves Him and what harms Him. I suspect that Isaiah is sensing what the Lord is sensing. The things that harm the Lord also harm the prophet. At this time, the Lord's people were no longer feeling their iniquity. They had become numb to sin and had rejected the love of God. Isaiah displays the heart of a prophet, one that corrects with tears in his eyes. He loved Israel enough to intercede every morning for them, despite the fact that they rejected the Lord's dominion over them. Isaiah reminded them each day who they were supposed to be. Morning by morning the prophet was appealing to Israel's conscience and he appeals to our conscience as well. This is the question we must ask: is our behavior opposing the One who longs to help us? That is why each day it is vital to awaken to the same summons as Isaiah. When we do, we free ourselves and others from indifference toward God and awaken to His strong sympathy toward us.

I'm absolutely convinced that to be a prophet we must see how seriously wounded the Lord's people are. Otherwise we won't stay alert and awake to the importance of what the Lord is saying. I am amazed at how much the Lord longs to tell us what to say and what to do, if we only give Him the opportunity. Isaiah gave his mornings to God and look at the impact and revelation the Lord gave him. Surely the Lord wants to do the same for us. And He will give us that same yearning that the prophet had, so that an entire company of men and women will look with expectation in the morning for the voice of God. No wonder Isaiah tells us what the Lord did for him, because I'm absolutely sure what the Lord said to Isaiah every morning was, "You can trust Me, Isaiah". How else would the prophet have been able to navigate his heart through many seemingly hopeless circumstances?

*"wakens my ear to listen like one being instructed." (Isaiah 50:4, NIV)*

The prophet is saying that he has learned to listen and that he never stops learning. Isaiah's life is a sign for prophetic inspiration. No matter how new we are or how seasoned we are, our obligation to the Lord is to yield to God's heart and soak up everything He desires to tell us. There are many sorts of activities going on in the world -- organizing, planning, legislating and a host of other things. But these concerns are only for man's existence in the world of time. God wants to give a generation the ear of a prophet. Because our mission is so dear to the Lord's heart. He wants us to become a people so locked into His plan that no one or nothing detours us from it. This phrase is of vital importance for our growth and maturity in the prophetic ministry because there is a tendency among prophetic people to launch out without really paying attention and without the proper training. This creates both confusion and rejection within the church.

We must get back to the art of listening and learning. And yes that happens when we are before the Lord, however it also happens within covenant community. By not being in covenant with other ministries the prophet can become autonomous. How many of us over the years have heard the words, "I hear from God, who are you to tell me what to do?" Individualism without community is what produces wrong doctrine. Within the context of church life, prophets have the wonderful opportunity to submit revelation to be discerned. This creates healthy relationships and causes the entire body of Christ to benefit from the prophet's message. The Lord has sovereignly allowed diversity to exist within the family of God so that all may grow in the art of hearing from God. This kind of submission to one another takes humility and a passion for patience. When that supervenes the prophet's supernatural experiences he or she is given a voice within church culture. At this present time the knowledge of God is increasing rapidly and those who are hungry will enroll in the same class has Isaiah did: "Here am I, send me".

Read Isaiah 50:4, *NIV*

Questions to ask

* What has the Lord given you to develop and how are you developing it?
* What does it mean to be well instructed?
* Have you ever given a word to someone who was weary or received a word when you were weary?
* What are our first thoughts when we wake up in the morning? God's voice or our trouble?
* How do we put ourselves in a posture of listening and learning?

Apprehending the truth

We can't help but stand in awe of this portion of scripture, it resonates with the passion to hear God's voice. It uncovers the prophet's desire to know God even after all he had experienced in his lifetime. Isaiah is communicating to us that learning from God never gets boring or old. And hearing from God keeps expectation alive. This removes the tension we feel at times when life seems disoriented. It also gives us a classroom for teaching the weak and weary what God has given us. And that's hope.

# CHAPTER FOUR

# WHO IS SURROUNDING ME

1 Kings 22:7, *NKJV*
*And Jehoshaphat said, Is there not still a prophet of the Lord here, that we may inquire of Him?*

2 Chronicles 20:20, *NKJV*
*Jehoshaphat stood and said, Hear me, O Judah and you inhabitants of Jerusalem: Believe in the Lord your God, and you shall be established; believe His prophets, and you shall prosper.*

One point is interesting to note in the life of King Jehoshaphat. When the enemy played upon his fears, this king immediately looked for a word from God. Jehoshaphat discovered a wonderful thing about the spirit of prophecy, that when we feel abandoned by family and friends, it causes us to realize how close we are to God and how much He cares, guides and protects. The ministry of the prophet reminds all of us just how committed the Lord is to our deepest concerns. For Jehoshaphat, God's word wasn't an option to be weighed out, it was life and death, blessing or captivity. Certainly we all can see why the Lord proved Himself in this King's life. What made Jehoshaphat great wasn't his army or his wealth. It was a sincere reliance upon the prophetic voice that the Lord had placed in his life.

Diligence and desperation are two sides of the same coin. The Lord used both to direct Jehoshaphat. This King understood that we need to inspire a nation to become desperate for God, and that takes a prophetic word. The Lord puts all of us in certain situations to inspire us and believe what is possible. The prophetic sets that in motion when we align our hearts and minds to the truth. Fear was not Jehoshaphat's anchor. By becoming desperate, Jehoshaphat gave the devil no chance. He didn't focus on his feelings and become filled with fear. The sense of urgency that was in his heart caused him to turn everything over to The Lord. In other words our response to life shows clear evidence to everyone what we choose to abide in. All of us have witnessed some in the body of Christ who abide in demonic activity or spiritual warfare but don't abide in Christ. Jehoshaphat didn't focus upon his feelings. He set himself to go after God. And when a group of believers corporately set themselves to seek the Lord and not their fears, God sends a word.

There is a genuine distinction between feeling fear and being filled with fear. Jehoshaphat chose not to abide in fear but to abide in the Lord. It's amazing that Jehoshaphat actually turned his fear into an asset; the fear caused him to desire to hear clearly from God. And whatever we abide in is what ultimately fills us. The Lord's greatness made Jehoshaphat great, made him brave, made him trust, made him love. I believe the Lord will do the same for us if we will hear His voice both individually and corporately. What will our posture be? May we learn from this great King and learn from what he chose to listen to.

Let's look closer at the story in 1 Kings 22:1-28, *NIV*:

*For three years there was no war between Aram and Israel. But in the third year Jehoshaphat king of Judah went down to see the king of Israel. The king of Israel had said to his officials, "Don't you know that Ramoth Gilead belongs to us and yet we are doing nothing to retake it from the king of Aram?" So he asked Jehoshaphat, "Will you go with me to fight against Ramoth Gilead?" Jehoshaphat replied to the king of Israel, "I am as you are, my people as your people, my horses as your horses." But Jehoshaphat also said to the king of Israel, "First seek the counsel of the Lord." So the king of Israel brought together the prophets—about four hundred men—and asked them, "Shall I go to war against Ramoth Gilead, or shall I refrain?" "Go," they answered, "for the Lord will give it into the king's hand." But Jehoshaphat asked, "Is there no longer a prophet of the Lord here whom we can inquire of?"*

*The king of Israel answered Jehoshaphat, "There is still one prophet through whom we can inquire of the Lord, but I hate him because he never prophesies anything good about me, but always bad. He is Micaiah son of Imlah. "The king should not say such a thing," Jehoshaphat replied. So the king of Israel called one of his officials and said, "Bring Micaiah son of Imlah at once." Dressed in their royal robes, the king of Israel and Jehoshaphat king of Judah were sitting on their thrones at the threshing floor by the entrance of the gate of Samaria, with all the prophets prophesying before them. Now Zedekiah son of Kenaanah had made iron horns and he declared, "This is what the Lord says: 'With these you will gore the Arameans until they are destroyed.'"*

*All the other prophets were prophesying the same thing. "Attack Ramoth Gilead and be victorious," they said, "for the Lord will give it into the king's hand." The messenger who had gone to summon Micaiah said to him, "Look, the other prophets without exception are predicting success for the king. Let your word agree with theirs, and speak favorably." But Micaiah said, "As surely as the Lord lives, I can tell him only what the Lord tells me." When he arrived, the king asked him, "Micaiah, shall we go to war against Ramoth Gilead, or not?" "Attack and be victorious," he answered, "for the Lord will give it into the king's hand." The king said to him, "How many times must I make you swear to tell me nothing but the truth in the name of the Lord?" Then Micaiah answered, "I saw all Israel scattered on the hills like sheep without a shepherd, and the Lord said, 'These people have no master. Let each one go home in peace.'" The king of Israel said to Jehoshaphat, "Didn't I tell you that he never prophesies anything good about me, but only bad?" Micaiah continued, "Therefore hear the word of the Lord: I saw the Lord sitting on his throne with all the multitudes of heaven standing around him on his right and on his left. And the Lord said, 'Who will entice Ahab into attacking Ramoth Gilead and going to his death there?' "One suggested this, and another that. Finally, a spirit came forward, stood before the Lord and said, 'I will entice him.' "By what means?' the Lord asked.*

*"'I will go out and be a deceiving spirit in the mouths of all his prophets,' he said.*

*"'You will succeed in enticing him,' said the Lord. 'Go and do it.'" So now the Lord has put a deceiving spirit in the mouths of all these prophets of yours. The Lord has decreed disaster for you." Then Zedekiah son of Kenaanah went up and slapped Micaiah in the face. "Which way did the spirit from the Lord go when he went from me to speak to you?" he asked. Micaiah replied, "You will find out on the day you go to hide in an inner room." The king of Israel then ordered, "Take Micaiah and send him back to Amon the ruler of the city and to Joash the king's son and say, 'This is what the king says: Put this fellow in prison and give him nothing but bread and water until I return safely.'" Micaiah declared, "If you ever return safely, the Lord has not spoken through me." Then he added, "Mark my words, all you people!"*

There is so much insight regarding the prophetic ministry in this story. It illustrates how different people react, discern and obey the word of the Lord. I love the fact that when Ahab's prophets were prophesying, Jehoshaphat speaks up. He questioned Ahab's prophets by asking Ahab for a prophet of the Lord. It seems to me that Jehoshaphat is really operating in the gift of discerning of spirits. One thing is clear, Ahab's prophets spoke out the intentions and purposes of their own hearts and not the heart of God. This teaches all of us to never prophesy out of our own intentions. Prophets are not to be political realists, they call individuals and nations back to total loyalty to the Lord. There seems to be a propensity in all of us, that when we feel threatened we turn toward political solutions rather than turning toward God and prayer. But when we are more interested in our individual rights than we are the truth, we become ensnared by the demonic.

Prophets at times are considered impractical because they are so extremely mindful of the things of God. They have been trained to see from the Lord's point of view. They have tapped into what God is interested in, withholding nothing. The prophet promotes God's will and by studying the works of God he becomes a voice to the thirsty and food for the hungry. However in the context of this story, the prophet is rejected by the political machine. It isn't that the prophet isn't concerned about what people think. It's just that for a prophet, what God thinks is most important. A prophet is commissioned to promote what God wills and not necessarily what public opinion wills.

The prophet never makes a treaty with spiritual recession. He deeply disturbs those who are living in compromise. Micaiah was not going to jeopardize eternity or principle in order to gain a following or to impress his listeners. We see from his example that a prophet isn't confused or upset when he faces ridicule, resistance, worldly opposition and even demonic assault! He stays true to the message. Every prophet must know the audience that he or she is addressing, however the Hebrew prophets never submitted to the audience. Instead, they passionately gave themselves to God, understanding that He was their audience. These Old Testament passages of scripture illustrate that the political spirit is really more concerned about rapport than it is about the prophetic word.

## Micaiah's epistle

King Ahab only surrounded himself with prophets that preached what he wanted to hear. We can see this same attitude demonstrated in the church when sects only surround themselves with prophets who speak what they agree with. This creates elitism, where ministry and ministers pride themselves in survival without simple trust in God. They exist for position but they neglect the presence of God. Micaiah (which means "who is like God") is summoned and we should all want the prophet who is like the Lord to speak. Not a prophet who represents a political party or agenda. But a prophet who is more concerned with relating to God correctly than being received or receiving praise from King Ahab.

When a person doesn't have the mind of God they will always come into agreement with what is appealing to the crowd and the majority. Their personal safety and popularity becomes the scale by which they judge their lives. Most of the time, being prophetically correct isn't the same as being politically correct. Sometimes preachers say what everyone else is saying, instead of what God is truly saying. Tragically these so-called prophets seem to align themselves with what everyone wants to hear. But being politically correct will economically bankrupt a nation. A true prophet doesn't speak for himself -- He speaks for the Lord.

Micaiah was in love with truth and we must be in love with truth also, no matter what it costs us. They wanted Micaiah to make a good showing before the King just like the other prophets did. However

God's prophet didn't seek his own glory. There are so many key principles in this story, but one of the most important is how easily all of can be swept along by hypocrisy or deception. I believe that the prophets who were prophesying victory for Ahab failed to consider the character of the king. Some may say, "But these were Jezebel's prophets ..." Before we say that, let's read the text through. I believe they really thought they were the Lord's prophets. What does this tell us today?

One word needs to define the next generation of prophets: Integrity. Why? Because true integrity has the ability to resist the pressures of popular opinions, whether social, cultural or political. Look at Micaiah, he didn't allow popular opinion to weaken his commitment. *This would be our epistle, our letter that everyone reads (II Cor. 3:2, NIV).* Even when this prophet wasn't accepted by the government or the church, he kept his heart right. Never growing bitter or afraid, he simply spoke what God said. If we are going to carry a prophetic mantle like Micaiah then whether we are endorsed or not, whether we are loved or hated, we must choose to be pure in our message because we love people! Micaiah and Jehoshaphat really were the only ones who loved King Ahab. Deception doesn't know how to love. It only knows how to take. Deception took Ahab's life but the Lord had sent a prophet to save it. If only Ahab had listened!

Let us look even deeper. Of course prophecy is to bring encouragement, strength and comfort, but it is never to promote rebellion. Micaiah honored Ahab's summons and delivered a word that no one else was willing to speak, yet he still honored the king. If the church is going to possess a prophetic culture, honor even in the midst of apostasy will have to characterize the people of God. This doesn't mean to reinterpret the scriptures or change what God says to fit our audience. It means even when we correct, we respect. It means we tell people that they need to bring themselves to a place of blessing. The prophet is to give people a road map back to God's favor. Remember what Micaiah told Ahab, "Let each return to his house in peace". Just like our current generation who are calling good evil and evil good, that's what Micaiah had to deal with. Lying had become the language of the religious system of Micaiah's day. Are we any different? May the Lord provoke the spirit of Micaiah in the hearts of preachers across the earth! People who are not frightened by political and religious structures that strike them or afflict them with philosophical beliefs. Because they still have the conviction that what will stand is the truth.

Read 1 Kings 22:1-28, *NIV*

Questions to ask

* What kind of people are we surrounding ourselves with? Those who are hearing God or those who don't care?
* What did Jehoshaphat do to overcome his fear when he was outnumbered?
* Have we made it a habit of hearing God through the prophetic ministry?
* Can we discern what is a deceptive prophecy from an authentic one?
* How should we posture ourselves to always align our hearts with truth?
* Will we allow the Spirit of God to be our hiding place by not giving in to the political and religious pressure of our day, like Micaiah?

Apprehending the truth

Micaiah and Jehoshaphat share a common characteristic and that is a love for what's real. Both of them really loved their nation even though Israel was filled with apprehension about its leaders and its prophets. Reading this story over the years has both encouraged me and filled me with more questions. For example, why do some people ask for the Lord's counsel when they have already decided what they are going to do? But the main thing it has done for me is cause me to pursue the voice of God in everything. Whether in the motionless and mundane or in the violent turbulence of life, it has delivered me from my fears. Because that's what God does. I pray it would do the same for you. And what a refreshing moment it is when a King and a prophet both love God with passionate sincerity!

# CHAPTER FIVE

# PROPHETIC WORSHIP

Ephesians 5:19, *NIV*
*speaking to one another in psalms and hymns and spiritual songs,*
*singing and making melody in your heart to the Lord*

As we begin this chapter I realize that in the body of Christ there is such a broad range of what is *called* worship and what really *is* worship. Many of the so-called sounds are simply personal preference rather than genuinely coming into the presence of Almighty God. Worship has become an industry rather than a lifestyle. Songs have been written and will continue to be written for entertainment under the guise of biblical worship. The influence of music has put some in bondage and has given comfort to others. You can't read scripture and not come to the understanding that God loves both music and worship.

God loves to sing and He loves sounds. God wrote the first song, "Let there be light" and all creation is still singing that song! What removes music away from God is the danger of human arrogance before His presence. This is very subtle because of an incorrect understanding of worship. For instance, Eli's sons were dissatisfied with their portion so they took what belonged to God (I Sam. 2:12-17, *NIV*). I believe that this is a lesson for all of us: we must be grateful for whatever portion the Lord has allocated to us. These sons used their authority as priests to even take by force the Lord's offering from the people of God. By neglecting what the Lord has demanded from us, we put people at risk. This is certainly true with Eli's sons. They had completely lost touch with what ministry was all about. By not honoring the authority of the Lord, Hophni and Phinehas adapted a leadership style of greed instead of generosity.

In other words, Eli's sons interfered with the worship by inhibiting the people of God to sacrifice unto the Lord. So what does this have to do with prophetic worship? We can see by reading the first three chapters of 1 Samuel that the word of the Lord was virtually nonexistent and there was a lack of spiritual vision. Why? Eli's sons stopped singing and stopped cultivating the prophetic spirit. This can happen to worship leaders, musicians and all of us for that matter. The worship leader stops singing to God and begins singing to a crowd or perhaps he becomes so intimidated that he holds back a song that could change the atmosphere.

Recently the Lord dropped into my spirit that many within the body of Christ are suffering from a "closed womb". They are experiencing closed doors, closed opportunities, closed supernatural interventions. Why? Because there was music but that music wasn't the "song of the Lord". So how do wombs get opened up? You know if you've been in a worship service that there are moments when it felt more like a C-section then an easy delivery. Not just because of lack of musical skill, but a lack of sensitivity to the presence of God. *This causes our structures to take precedence over Paul's exhortation to sing spiritual songs.* Prophecy opens wombs and when we begin to couple prophecy with anointed music, we will have a culture that stops complaining and cursing, and starts making a melody in their heart to the Lord! I am absolutely sure that when the prophetic word is sung, it restores dignity and identity to those who receive it. We must understand that our ministry position, whatever it may be, is temporal. But our position as a worshipper is forever. Obviously the truth of who God is should be our source. Yet what Paul writes in Ephesians 5:19 should be the well that worship leaders, prophets and the people of God draw from. Let's take a closer look :

*"speaking to one another" (Ephesians 5:19, NIV)*

Prophetic worship is really repeating what the Lord said or is saying at the moment. According to this verse (and other passages in the Word of God) our speech should have a prophetic dimension. This means that when we talk to each other and sing before each another the wells of the spirit flow out of us. What we say and how we say it, is so important if we want to have prophetic authority. Authority is our realm of influence. Singing the right song can usher us into a realm of the spirit that releases people from all kinds of bondages and sickness, where they experience salvation and forgiveness.

By submitting to the Lord, we enlarge our authority and the Kingdom of God begins to become visible. For instance, one phrase spoken under the Holy Spirit's authority has the potential to arrest those who have never submitted themselves to Jesus. The reign of God fully begins to manifest as the servants of His Kingdom submit themselves fully to its government. That is when the Kingdom comes with authority and power! When people begin to sense God's presence, they are moved to respond, because they were created to respond to the Lord. However our tendency is to get through the song service but never camp out in the place of God's presence. Spontaneous worship allows believers and nonbelievers to pitch themselves in the Lord's tabernacle. Then the Holy Spirit begins to move freely among the people and do what none of us could do, even on our best day. When men and women begin to lift their eyes toward Heaven, right thinking is restored. Only when a people, a nation, an individual lifts their eyes to Heaven will right thinking and understanding return.

I'm convinced that if we are going to be a prophetic people that our deficiencies cannot be our frequency. In other words, by speaking with one another we see collectively the dignity of others. The song of the Lord fills hearts with dignity and as God's mercy brushes over us, our emotions get touched and our minds get renewed. The world doesn't speak this way to each other. But the Lord is moving upon the church to speak the language that awakens dignity. I believe it's time to speak!

*"in psalms and hymns and spiritual songs" (Ephesians 5:19, NIV)*

Sacredness is found in the psalms, the sacredness for His house, His acts, His mercy. No one in scripture knew the sacredness of God like David. How was that cultivated, how was it played out in practice? One thing is for sure: the psalms touch every emotion you and I will ever have. It removes the idol of hypocrisy, which is sacrilege, which means "the violation and misuse of that which is sacred". This is religion without the Lord. The apostle tells us that those who don't fear God don't see the Lord as their necessity. When there is no fear of God before our eyes, our religious activities become just sacrilege. And sacrilege attempts to redefine truth on its own terms -- nothing is sacred but its own ideas. Without the fear of God, we subvert our own happiness. I believe the reason why the apostle wrote this verse to the church of Ephesus was to train and exhort them to recognize the cultural idolatry surrounding the church.

As believers we are to speak the word of God over each other. This is completely opposite of the religious tabloids that spread the church's dirt. We must become like Noah's two sons who honored and respected their father's authority. This should be the heart's attitude toward those who make mistakes, both small and large. These two sons put a robe over their shoulders and walked backwards in order to cover their father's nakedness. But Noah's son Ham spoke a language that was revealing, spreading the latest gossip regarding his father's drunkenness. This is completely opposite of psalms, hymns and spiritual songs.

I believe that in a prophetic culture, we come to church with a robe over our shoulder. This frees us from slandering others when they do things we don't agree with. Let's make it our goal to keep the name of God holy in our midst so He might release greater power. Those who are rebellious want spiritual leaders to fall into sin instead of being blessed by God. They have lost the ability to be captivated by God, so to cover their boredom they turn to slander. Slander is the language of the offended. That's why Paul called us to sing and prophesy over each other because psalms, hymns and spiritual songs repair the soul.

*"singing and making melody in your heart to the Lord" (Ephesians 5:19, NIV)*

I believe that when we respond according to these words we learn to bear the opposition of others. We begin to detect our own shortcomings, our own condition and thus eliminate any criticism of others. What is the melody of the prophet? Singing before the Lord both corporately and privately connects us to the throne of Heaven, making us more aware of the presence of God. Worshipping produces a conscience that is extremely sensitive to the movements of the Holy Spirit. The more we make a melody in our hearts to the Lord, the more we acquire a taste for Jesus' life. And His life was a continual song before His Father. Jesus found a rhythm in everything He did. That rhythm was obedience. Paul and Silas found the rhythm in a prison cell and everyone heard their song and found their chains falling off. What melody are you and I singing? A song that is building up or a song about our troubles?

Our song can potentially restrict us or free us. By making a melody of gratitude we will find ourselves standing before His presence and watching Him answer our prayers and prophetic decrees. For He reigns over everything and anyone. Let's agree with what the apostle instructed and not sit in the pew and whine. By singing we pour out our hearts to Him, which invites the cloud of His glory to hover over each one of us. By singing we release joy in the atmosphere, peace in the mind and grace upon the heart!

That is what Jesus did for the woman at the well. He showed her which well to draw from and when she found that well she got herself into the rhythm of deliverance. She sang a song prophetically over an entire city and they all came to the Author of her song! Jesus stayed two more days singing over people who no one thought were worthy, preaching to those who everyone had written off. What happened? Revival!

Don't you agree, that Paul touched on why the church needs to sing? Because when we sing, the Lord comes into our midst. He saves souls, heals bodies, awakens hearts, adds to the church and empowers the congregation. We the church possess the melody that the world longs to hear! It is time, like never before, for our prophetic culture to sing over the nations and the needs of humanity to give them a glimpse of Heaven.

Read Ephesians 5:19, *NIV*

Questions to ask

- * What does prophetic worship look like to me?
- * Why did the Apostle Paul tell the church of Ephesus to speak to one another in psalms and hymns and spiritual songs?

* In what ways can we both individually and corporately encourage prophetic singing?
* Has the current church structure fallen away from this mandate by Paul? If so how can we get it back and make it a part of our culture?
* When looking at the rhythm of Jesus' life, how can we find that same rhythm?
* In my private life, do I make time to make melody in my heart to the Lord?

Apprehending the truth

Paul is telling us how to sing prophetically. The more we implement what he said, the more natural it becomes. Praise flows out of a heart that is on fire before the Lord. Both creativity and music are a gift from our Creator. When we mix them together, something explosive starts to happen! The language of Heaven gets introduced to an entire generation. Like Paul, we are all instructors attempting to teach someone our melody. Which melody are you teaching? Our words demonstrate the song that is playing within our soul. Every moment of every day we have to choose what we listen to and what we choose to repeat. I think we should learn from the apostle and discover the language that can change our hearts.

# CHAPTER SIX

# WHAT IS THE
# PROPHET'S REWARD?

Isaiah 49:4, *NIV*
*But I said, "I have labored in vain; I have spent my strength for
nothing at all. Yet what is due me is in the Lord's hand, and my
reward is with my God."*

No matter how mature we are, there are times when discouragement
and disappointment confront us. Those who are in a prophetic
culture are especially susceptible, partly because of our idealism
and partly because of our legitimate promises from God over many
years. The prophet Isaiah finds himself in this place. Arguably the
most articulate and the most prolific writer of the Old Testament,
and speaks more about the coming of the Messiah than any other
prophet. His encounter at the throne of God which mirrors John's
book of Revelation is stunning. Yet in this verse we see the human
side of one of the greatest prophets that ever lived. I want to explore
that side because we too share in Isaiah's struggle. This struggle is
to tell a nation to turn back to God when they are truly not interested
in how God thinks and feels. I didn't say they weren't interested in
religion – because everyone is to some degree.

Isaiah loved Israel – that is very clear in his writings. I don't believe for a moment that the prophet was indifferent or immune to what the people were experiencing. He wept within himself for the leaders who refused to listen to God's word and for the rest of Israel who ignored him. I've taken this verse because we can learn much from what Isaiah feels and how he overcomes. Highs and lows are part of our human existence, but they don't mean that we're unstable or not redeemable. They teach us about God and about ourselves. Our priorities can easily get redefined by an incorrect source of joy. Our perspective can get blurred by what our roles are and how we might accomplish the assignment the Lord has for us. I'm sure that Isaiah felt that life was too crowded with religious gamesmanship and political maneuvering. Maybe he even lost his voice during the sermon, sensing that his impact as a prophet was diminishing. Isaiah attempted to walk with God when no one else around him was. When we find ourselves in a similar situation we can feel demoralized, like our work for the Lord has little value. And just like in Isaiah's time, so it is in our time, fear is at an epidemic stage. There is a much-needed lesson in Isaiah's preaching: "make God your sole allegiance". No one else and nothing else. Because we have a tendency to trip over what offends us.

*"I have labored in vain; I have spent my strength for nothing at all." (Isaiah 49:4, NIV)*

This is an explosive emotional bombshell that the prophet is making before the Lord. "I've labored in vain." What did he just say? Am I reading this right? It is raw and real and everyone has felt this way at one time or another. The wise will observe not only the character of God but also the character of the prophet. Since listening is the primary way to obtain wisdom, not just listening to anything, but listening to what God is saying. Many pastors and ministry leaders feel that the work they do is useless or for no purpose. It seems they have expended a lot of energy for absolutely nothing. So then depression sets in, along with apathy and a prayerless life, even in the midst of seemingly outward success. What is the answer?

The pressure on the outside caused the prophet Isaiah to incorrectly evaluate his ministry. So we see that we can derail our labor if our mind isn't renewed. And we can easily feel that our labor is of no value if we have lost the supernatural element. We believe that because we have been called by God that the people will accept what we bring to the table. But the prophet often feels the pain of not being accepted by the very people he is called to. The Lord is teaching us here that we will never ascend through self-analysis, and never arrive at the right destination in our hearts when we compare our labor.

There is a lack of wholeness in the body of Christ because we've misplaced what is sacred, what is real reverence and honor. A prophetic culture has learned that their efforts are so much different than the efforts of unbelievers. Every leader needs to acknowledge that there are people who will enforce their leadership and others who will resist their leadership. Yes, there are moments when we all feel that we lack the resources to secure life, yet there is One who we may call upon -- His name is Jesus! Our authority as a leader may be challenged, but when we fall face down asking for grace and mercy, no one will be able to disable us. When we the church do not consider our destiny we relinquish our authority. If this can happen to Isaiah, surely we can get ourselves into the same situation. Part of seeking God is making ourselves vulnerable to being wounded and yet continuing to pursue God's will. Excuses were doing their best to create a deep wound in the prophet's soul. But our wounds and our offenses shouldn't change our behavior because we are so hungry for His presence. I remember the Lord speaking this to my spirit, "Is ministry success the only display of My love for you? Or is My peace, My grace and My patience in your weakness?"

*"Yet what is due me is in the Lord's hand, and my reward is with my God." (Ephesians 5:19, NIV)*

What is due us isn't in the hands of others. It is in the hand of God and this truth must resonate in our hearts because of the world we live in. We live in a world where many feel a sense of entitlement because of their personal condition. That is simply not true, because our greatest wage is knowing the Lord's presence. A sincere knowledge that what is in the Lord's hand is my greatest source of fulfillment and pleasure. Isaiah comes to this conclusion despite unfortunate events surrounding his life. In ministry there are so many that work so diligently. Yet they feel that because of all the energy they expend, they can expect a reward. This mindset can sometimes produce an incorrect expectation that causes burnout, anxiety and a variety of other spiritual and emotional ills. Our incorrect ideas about what may be due to us can severely limit our ability to receive the wealth that the Lord possesses. We need to understand that what has been reserved for us is really right in front of us. And when we recognize what has been kept for us it moves our heart to obey. This puts a longing in our hearts to have Jesus completely rule over everything.

While some unconsciously declare independence from the Lord by their individual choices, we choose never to drown ourselves in a sugarcoated gospel. Whatever the people choose to do or not do isn't my reward, God is. My reward is not with people, it is with God. He is the One who determines my effectiveness. For my ultimate reward is not in the hands of people. My greatest reward is not popularity, economic success, doors of opportunity and the like. My greatest reward is being with my God. Then the word "reward" takes on a whole new meaning, which is being completely at peace. In other words, the prophet receives the revelation that he can be absolutely at peace even when he is rejected.

Do we desire the Lord's presence with such intensity that even if we are not received it doesn't matter? Pressures from the outside caused the prophet Isaiah to incorrectly evaluate his ministry. He felt that he was wasting his oxygen on these people. Because there was no response, no reaction, no effect. Do you feel the prophet's heart? When Jesus is our reward, rejection can't make us miserable. What you don't respect, you don't receive. You can't just read this verse -- you have to feel it. Isaiah realizes whose servant he really is. Who am I allowing to influence me – the people or heaven?

Man always discredits what he doesn't receive. They didn't receive Jesus, because instead of pursuing God they pursued their own imaginations. Many are rejected because of their appearance because they don't fit the description of a prophet. However the prophetic culture that is arising doesn't fit in to anyone's ideals except the Lord. And just like Isaiah they have rebounded and resounded, to be completely free from fitting in. They burn to be a voice, to experience fully what has been written and prophesied about them. Let us all come to recognize what Isaiah recognized so we can recover our hearts and the heart of a generation.

Read Isaiah 49:4, *NIV*

Questions to ask

* Have you ever felt that your work for the Lord was insignificant?
* Were you ever in a spiritual place of burnout and ineffectiveness?
* What was the one truth that produced an understanding that what really is due to you, isn't determined by others?

* Have you gotten to a place where rejection may hurt, but it doesn't cripple?
* What revelation stood out in this verse that empowered you to overcome?
* What can we glean from Isaiah's honesty and vulnerability?

Apprehending the truth

Scripture is filled with beautiful expressions and liberating truth. Yet this verse has thundered throughout my years in ministry. We must understand that whether we are influencing a few or multitudes, it all comes back to this question. Why? What is my reward? God loves to reward His children. We are so grateful for the healings, the miracles, the prophetic words that have gone forth. Salvations, deliverances and sermons. Yet we see that this prophet puts everything back into right perspective. God is my Father and your Father. He is intimately involved, working on others while working on us. It is so freeing to know that no matter how seemingly small or large we become before others, Jesus is right there laboring alongside us. The prophet discovered this when he was under pressure and his transparency encourages us when we find ourselves in the same circumstances. We all desperately need to take hold of the same burning perspective of this man of God: nothing is lost when He is with me.

# CHAPTER SEVEN

# RECALIBRATING WHAT IS ESSENTIAL

Psalm 74:9, *NKJV*
*We do not see our signs; There is no longer any prophet; Nor is there any among us who knows how long.*

The church has both the greatest history and the greatest future. But why in the development of a prophetic culture would we need to highlight this passage of scripture? Certainly the writer of Psalm 74 is revealing to us that his spiritual environment is at a dangerous level. Religious pollutants had crept their way in and now the church was doing ministry without the signs of God's power. They had reduced the gospel to something social rather than authentically supernatural. This was easy for leadership because it required little passion and limited commitment.

Psalms 74:9, *NET*
*We do not see any signs of God's presence; there are no longer any prophets and we have no one to tell us how long this will last. We do not see our signs*

The Lord is the source of signs and signs are to be demonstrated throughout the church. Signs are the authentication of genuine

Christianity. In other words, we must have a work done inside of us that only the Lord Almighty can do.

## FIVE THINGS THAT HAD BEEN IN SOLOMON'S TEMPLE WERE NO LONGER THERE:

### 1 – ARK OF THE COVENANT

Anointing upon the word

John 4:32,34 (NKJV)

*But He said to them, "I have food to eat of which you do not know." 34. Jesus said to them, "My food is to do the will of Him who sent Me, and to finish His work.*

John 4:31, *NKJV*
*In the meantime His disciples urged Him, saying, "Rabbi, eat."*

John 4:32, *NKJV*
*But He said to them, "I have food to eat of which you do not know."*

John 4:33, *NKJV*
*Therefore the disciples said to one another, "Has anyone brought Him anything to eat?"*

John 4:34, *NKJV*
*Jesus said to them, "My food is to do the will of Him who sent Me, and to finish His work."*

### 2 - FIRE ON THE ALTAR

Prayer and worship are a lifestyle and not just a moment

## 3 - SHEKINAH CLOUD OF HIS PRESENCE

1 Kings 18:41, *NKJV "Then Elijah said to Ahab, "Go up, eat and drink; for there is the sound of abundance of rain."*

We can clearly see Ahab's "anchor" is pleasure and not revival.

The prophet exposes the priorities of the world -- eating and drinking. The people don't understand the urgency of the hour or the essential need for rain.

The prophet perceived that something tiny in size would become something large.

1 Kings 18:42, *NKJV*
*So Ahab went up to eat and drink. And Elijah went up to the top of Carmel; then he bowed down on the ground, and put his face between his knees,*

Have we humbled ourselves? Have we been willing to make ourselves uncomfortable?

The prophet understood the urgency of the situation.
The church is eating and drinking while the prophet understands the essential need for rain (revival).

It's only when we press into the presence of God that we begin to see the possibility of rain.

Have we given our attention to The Lord or to our eating and drinking? There needs to be a sense of urgency in the church. I don't think we have the urgency of the prophet Elijah. We must go beyond everyone else in order to believe for an outpouring.

## 4 - URIM AND THUMMIM

Job 22:28, *AMP*
*You shall also decide and decree a thing, and it shall be established for you; and the light [of God's favor] shall shine upon your ways.*

## 5 - SPIRIT OF PROPHECY

Prophecy had been suspended by teachers who said we don't need it anymore.

Without the spirit of prophecy there is no originality. So we can become guilty of plagiarism. Plagiarism means to imitate the language and thoughts of others. Without the spirit of prophecy, we don't have to rely upon the Holy Spirit for revelation -- we get our revelation from others.

A plagiarist is a thief, a pirate. That is why we have copyright laws.

Daniel 12:4, *NKJV*
*But you, Daniel, shut up the words, and seal the book until the time of the end; many shall run to and fro, and knowledge shall increase.*

Because of men's ability to travel across the earth to and fro we see this prophecy being fulfilled. We see knowledge increasing yet the revelation of God is decreasing.

Without the gift of prophecy, political correctness is the theme which is preached from the pulpit.

# FIVE THINGS THAT TAKE PLACE IN SOCIETY BEFORE REVIVAL BREAKS OUT:

1) greed and increase in crime
2) corruption in politics and business practices
3) perversion becomes mainstream
4) occultic domination
5) increase in anti-biblical sentiment

# CHAPTER EIGHT

# DECISION, DECREE, DESTINATION

Job 22:28, AMP
*You shall also decide and decree a thing, and it shall be established*
*for you; and the light [of God's favor] shall shine upon your ways.*

*"You shall also decide" (Amp)*

There is not a shortage of dreams within the church, but there is
often a lack of concrete decisions to see those dreams come to pass.
For without a clear vision there is no passion to pursue our goals.
Decisions will keep our hearts focused. The good news is that those
who have made determined resolutions will consistently rehearse
the goodness of God in their minds. They've come to the conclusion
that happiness means being completely occupied by the Lord and
not by other things. This truth strengthens their resolve and their
commitment to their choices.

The reason I have decided to unpack this scripture in Job is to
encourage you not to just sit and wait for the Lord to do something.
He has already done everything! He is just waiting for us to stop
using "waiting on God" as the reason for our procrastination. Many
people are extremely gifted, anointed and even called, but they

are afraid to make a commitment to their dreams. So they become specialists in echoing words of regret. They watch others do great things for God and even though they have tremendous talent, they waste it by postponing their desires. They use excuses like, "I don't have the money, the education or the opportunities".

Indecision has a crippling power because it requires absolutely no faith. We must decide to pursue the benefits and blessings that the Lord has made available. We must resist the temptation to second guess ourselves and instead respond with a sense of purpose. Our decisions are the mirror reflection of our words. Choices are made every day that determine how much light we allow into our lives. I believe there is always the tendency to analyze so much that we fail to make concrete judgements. However, using our weapons of prayer and proclamation will reinforce our ability to make wise choices. Then as we make purposeful decisions, we experience the success we long for. Although none of us is fully aware of what the future holds, many of us have the privilege to choose what kind of life we want to live. This is why I believe this promise is in God's word. *You shall also decide ... it shall be established for you.*

Beloved, we need prophetic sons and daughters to equip the body of Christ to recognize that they have been given a backbone. We see this demonstrated throughout the holy scriptures. One example is the story of Jonathan and his armorbearer. They were outnumbered and had very few weapons, but through a decision to fight for the Lord, God gave them a great victory (I Samuel 14:1-23). Creative people don't allow fear to stop them from their resolve. As they take steps of faith, they attract others who are willing to help them accomplish their dreams. This kind of culture is what makes up a healthy church. Purposes then become realities instead of just discussions around the table! We discover how much God yearns to fulfill the desires in our hearts. By making righteous choices we literally expel everything that is negative and we find beauty and delightfulness in our relationship with the Lord.

*"and decree a thing" (AMP)*

Everything the Lord speaks will come to pass and we have been authorized by His grace to decree the things that He has decreed. Announcing what the Lord has said indicates our belief that we will receive what we have spoken. At times we all drift away from the center, but godly speech can get us right back on point as we speak what the Lord has proclaimed. So difficulties become an opportunity for us to decree, instead of becoming buried under our circumstances. When we are disturbed we must ask ourselves, does the disturbance affect our decisions even to the point of disobeying the Lord? Situations can get very dark if anxiety takes over our obedience. The things we feed on will eventually become what we delight in. I passionately believe that by making prophetic decrees we actually impregnate earth with heaven's value system. Truth is what shapes values, not lies. And prophetic decrees are preemptive strikes against anything that would attempt to oppose God.

The prophetic culture is intentional about extending the rule of heaven. What is the rule of heaven? It is the great commission, the healing of bodies and the deliverance from demonic power. These signs occur because we have been given the privilege to decree the word of the Lord. We must have the same voice that was crying in the wilderness. The same tone of desperation and love. The same sound of conviction and compassion. That voice awakens in all of us what is real and what is pure. It will free our souls from cultural propaganda and the boredom of organized religion.

This brings us to the brook of Elijah (1 Kings 17:2-7). The brook was there to teach the prophet to rely upon resources outside himself. Yet it also teaches that the brook is never a long-term resource, because it eventually dries up. Ravens naturally eat meat and do not give it away, yet the Lord's command changed the order of nature to provide for his people. The brook and the ravens demonstrate how much God loves those who know His voice. And when His voice is the primary source of our provision, we become a people who are led and not driven. Then the church will discern the distinctions that accompany an outpouring of the Spirit of God. Prophetic words will become a part of the culture of the church. A greater vision of the majesty of Jesus will impregnate the congregation. The body of Christ will corporately become connected with God's dream for humanity. A deep respect for the young, the old, men and women regardless of status or stature will define the church. Undeniable signs and wonders that awaken people to God's presence and power will be upon many people. All because of a decree.

*"And it shall be established for you." (AMP)*

To be established is to confirm, to fulfill and to make good. This promise from God's Word is the Lord's covenant announcement to those who decree what the heart of God is saying. The church has been built and established so that the gates of hell don't completely destroy society. It's easier to lean upon government when we feel threatened, but it takes sincere faith to lean upon the Lord. This is not just true when faced with a military threat but also when faced with an economic one. The stories in scripture regarding God's intervention are to be the foundation on which we build our lives. This allows us the wonderful opportunity to learn to trust God in our personal experiences. Although the Lord has ordained government, He desires that we build on a genuine understanding of His heart. Otherwise we step beyond our authority (our realm of influence), and in doing so, we actually establish a demonic kingdom rather than the Kingdom of God. In a prophetic culture we all need to recognize our realm of authority. Otherwise we can mimic the Pharisees, who washed their hands but never washed their hearts. They prepared themselves to go to church, but failed to prepare themselves to worship. They had lips that spoke about God but possessed a heart that wasn't in love with God. This is not the way our Lord calls us to live! May our souls feel the words of our Lord Jesus and yearn for an outpouring of the Holy Spirit.

One truth must burn in a prophetic culture: the presence of divine intervention establishes those who are truly called of God. In other words, signs from heaven are how the Lord establishes His favor and power. The heart of a true prophetic movement must not be established by human endorsement, but by a love for purity and the presence of God. We don't establish ourselves, the Lord does, and He uses the church to confirm the call on our lives. All of us yearn to be elevated to the status of greatness, and some in the church would call that arrogance. However, the Lord never corrected the disciples for desiring to be great, He showed them how. Mark 10:43 *Yet it shall not be so among you; but whoever desires to become great among you shall be your servant.* I think this is one of the most amazing verses in scripture. Jesus doesn't destroy their desire for greatness, He affirms it. I believe that the Lord wants to establish His greatness in the lives of His people as we choose to serve Him and others.

*"And the light [of God's favor] shall shine upon your ways". (AMP)*

My wife and I met on the island of Maui and lived there for twenty years. There was a beautiful hotel near our home that sat beside the beach. I remember one evening we decided to walk down to the beach from that hotel. It was dark outside, but along the concrete steps were lights that lit our path. The lights had been strategically placed all along the steps and the beautiful landscape. Every time I read this verse it brings back that memory. I believe that the Lord plants light alongside our destinies, to help us go where He wants to take us. He empowers our minds with wisdom and revelation so that we can love like He loves and live like He lives. But this can't happen unless we have light. My heart burns for more revelation and to experience the light of God's favor, not only in ministry but in every area of life. This divine favor will clear a pathway for us all to walk in His peace, even when there is darkness around us.

What does it mean to have God shine on your ways? It means that you don't have to react to the darkness because your steps are illuminated and you have no fear of stumbling. When we live in the light, we never have to be afraid of the unknown because our course has been set by His favor. Do you need God to shine on your ways? I believe you do. When He shines upon us, darkness loses its power to draw us into fear. We take God at His word and simply serve Him and watch Him work for us.

As I study the book of First Samuel, I can't help but think about King Saul and how the Lord wanted so much to shine upon him. But it is startling to read that the Lord regretted making Saul king. Why? Because the Lord could never establish disobedience and pretense. Saul seemed to continually excuse his mistakes and never truly repented. But repentance establishes our credibility with God and gets us back on the path where the light is shining. The Lord shines upon the broken and the humble. When we look at people who are broken and meek we will see that God's favor and light keeps them on the narrow path that leads to life.

Read Job 22:28 & 1 Samuel 15 (NKJV)

Questions to ask:

* When making decisions do I make them according to my opinions and experiences or for "love's sake"?
* Who and what has shaped my decisions the most?

* Where could I improve the most regarding my speech?
* What kind of language am I speaking over my circumstances?
* Where do I need God's favor most? Family? Spirituality? Economically?
* When looking over your life, where has the Lord shined the greatest? In what ways has He guided you?

Apprehending the truth

For my wife and I, this verse in Job has become a "life verse". The Holy Spirit has used this portion of scripture to lead us to our destination. Beloved, a variety of books have been written on success but I believe that true success begins with a decision to affect eternity. The anointing upon our lives doesn't give us permission to promote ourselves, the anointing gives us permission to listen to the voice of God. We will never get to our destination without being good listeners. No matter how much we think we know, we should never stop listening. We should always beware of making ourselves autonomous when it comes to listening to the voice of the Lord. Certainly history proves that listening to Jesus is greater than any other activity.

# CHAPTER NINE

# WHICH VOICE IS PREVAILING?

Luke 23:23, NKJV
*But they were insistent, demanding with loud voices that He be crucified. And the voices of these men and of the chief priests prevailed.*

Unfortunately, King Saul and Pilate share some of the same leadership tendencies. We see that every leader is put to the same test: What voices will you be influenced by? The thing that we choose to give our attention to determines our future and the future of those who we influence. Many times leaders are more concerned about "saving face" in front of people than actually saving the people. Yet every prophetic leader needs to be deeply in touch with the attitudes of others. Saying things like, "I don't care what they think" or "Don't pay attention to those people" is simply a sign of immaturity. In contrast, those who are deeply in love with God don't want even the disobedient o be dishonored.

I think both King Saul and Pilate found themselves extremely divided over what to do when conflict arose. This stems from a divided heart which knows the truth yet operates out of the fear of man. In the face of conflict, both of these leaders chose to withdraw from the Lord. When that happens, a person becomes unpredictable. Both King Saul and Pilate became indecisive, which caused their vision to become distorted. As they withdrew, they were drawn further into the demonic. Whatever voice is prevailing is the voice that we yield to. And without wholeheartedness the pressure of the voices of violence usually win. People put demands on every leader, yet when the demands of the people attempt to override God's commands, the leader should never yield to the crowd. When a leader lacks clarity and confidence he may try to cash in on popularity and fail to glorify God.

*So Pilate, wanting to gratify the crowd, released Barabbas to them; and he delivered Jesus, after he had scourged Him, to be crucified.* Mark 15:15, NKJV

We show our lust for political acceptance when we cater to the crowd. As conflict arose, Pilate got caught up in the snare of his own personal ambition. On the other hand, it seems that Saul was constantly drawn away from who he was called to be. I Samuel 14:19 says, *Now it happened, while Saul talked to the priest, that the noise which was in the camp of the Philistines continued to increase; so Saul said to the priest, "Withdraw your hand."* (NKJV) When the noise increased, Saul became more preoccupied with the Philistines at the expense of calling upon God. He ended his conversation with God in order to engage with the Philistines. When the 'noise' increases, leaders sometimes have a tendency to increase their ministry efforts instead of seeking the Lord for guidance. It is vital to understand that prophecy gives us a profound sense of destiny. Without this sense of destiny, we have the tendency to withdraw from the presence of God. King Saul demonstrated his true character when he withdrew from asking the priest for divine guidance. It's as if Saul is saying, "I want to do what I want, so please withdraw Your hand." When conflicts and distractions surrounded him, he stopped seeking God. Neither Saul nor Pilate understood this principle lesson: all of us should be motivated by a sense of eternity and not just a sense of urgency.

We so desperately need to understand that gifted people can begin to cater to the rich and powerful, while neglecting the call to be poor in spirit. I want to emphasize that all of us who love the prophetic must maintain a poverty of spirit. To be poor in spirit is to be destitute and helpless and conscious of our spiritual need. When we understand the depth of our need for God, we become prosperous. To be poor in spirit is to become like the prophet who said, "I am undone" and to understand our need for guidance. Did the voice of the crowd drown out the voice of Pilate's conscience? Or had his conscience already been perverted? Was Saul's self-image so fractured that he couldn't find himself, so he looked to others for affirmation instead of looking for God? Oh how shallow and weak Pilate's leadership was, that he allowed himself to be so influenced by hatred instead of justice! Saul's priority was finding his significance in what people thought of him instead of what God thought of him. Whose voice is prevailing? The voice of humanity changes like the weather, it shouts for its rights, it destroys and it demands. At times we all feel extreme pressure emotionally, relationally, economically and physically. But the loving voice of God is available to talk, to counsel, to instruct, to encourage, to give hope, to correct and to affirm.

Let's look at another verse in the scripture. John 18:39 *"But you have a custom that I should release someone to you at the Passover. Do you therefore want me to release to you the King of the Jews?" (NKJV)* The word "custom" stands out in this verse. In this context, it means an established habit. However, all of us need to ask what is the source or origin of a particular custom. Sometimes what sounds extremely compassionate could really be evil, depending upon its origin. A demonstration of compassion is not always a reflection of tenderheartedness. A crowd pleaser may use compassion as a means to manipulate.

Pilate believed that he had the authority to control the destiny of Jesus! When the church operates through policy and fails to operate in Kingdom principles, they believe that they have control over the destinies of others. There are people in leadership who only lead in order to control and there are others who operate in love and truth. Which one will we be? Pilate chose policy over the truth that was made available to him through God's mercy. It was a policy that crucified our Lord Jesus. That is why I'm so passionate to establish a prophetic culture that is moved by the word of the Lord and not by human polices that are merely traditions. Beloved, don't ever allow policy to supersede biblical principles! What is amazing about Pilate is that he could have chosen not to be involved in the crucifixion of our Lord. Matthew 27:19 *While he was sitting on the judgment seat, his wife sent to him, saying, "Have nothing to do with that just Man, for I have suffered many things today in a dream because of Him".* *(NKJV)* Even though Pilate didn't have a relationship with the Lord, his closest human relationship was with his wife. She was the only one who could speak to him in this way. Others would have been terrified to confront him, yet she was doing all she could to rescue her husband from madness. I am fully persuaded that her dream was a prophetic warning from God. It was the mercy of God reaching out to Pilate. But Pilate desired to gratify the crowd more than he desired to obey the prophetic word through the dream.

There are a number of spiritual and life lessons we can learn from this narrative. When faced with conflict it is easier to lean upon policies and traditions than to lean upon prophetic revelation. It takes absolutely no faith to function from the place of tradition. On the other hand, functioning from dreams, visions and prophetic words takes a much more authentic faith. This kind of attitude pleases God. Pilate represents worldly authority and government which operates in accordance with men's structures and not Kingdom structures. Pilate could have done what his wife told him to do: *Have nothing to do with this "just" man.* The Lord had revealed to her that Jesus was truly innocent of every accusation. But when we reject the truth, we forfeit our rights for any further revelation. Pilate believed that truth was debatable. He believed that a dialogue between both parties was necessary, so he questioned the Lord. When society sees truth as a subject of debate rather than something to simply be received, it will choose to crucify the very thing it needs to conform to. Pilate feared offending the Jews more than he feared offending God.

Without truth, man begins to live like an animal, obeying only his instincts without taking thought of a righteous God. John the Baptist preached: *"He must increase, He I must decrease."* But for Saul it was the opposite: "I must increase and God must decrease". The need for public honor was more important to Saul than being fully committed to the Lord's honor. Saul fed his fears, which began to assault his assurance in the prophet Samuel's words. Without a zeal for God's presence we cultivate a deformed self-image, because we are not living to be conformed into *His* image. When we take such a position, we are choosing self-image over His image. One truth is clearly seen in Saul: "my value as an individual depends on what others think of me". 1 Samuel 15:30 *Then he said, "I have sinned; yet honor me now, please, before the elders of my people and before Israel, and return with me, that I may worship the Lord your God."* (NKJV) Every person has the desire to feel important, but Saul was recognized as important in the eyes of his people but not his God. Are we getting our feeling of significance from others or from God Himself? Saul had lost his honor before the Lord so the only thing he had left was to be honored before people. John 12:43 *"For they loved the praise of men more than the praise of God"* (NKJV)

Our self-worth shouldn't depend upon our position in life. Our self-worth has already been demonstrated by Christ's death on the cross. King Saul's self-worth was completely defined by how he was perceived by others. It should have been based upon the truth that he had been chosen by the Lord. Saul had so much potential but he limited his obedience to God to his own definition. This left him completely open to fear and deep depression. Why? Because his own voice prevailed over the voice of God. We who long for the prophetic must intercede like never before through fasting and a purity of lifestyle, living entirely for the glory of God. Our prayer should be that God's voice would prevail in every system and structure and that men and women around the earth would obey.

Read Matthew 27, NKJV

Questions to ask:

* Were there times in your life when the pressure to please others caused you to miss God's voice?
* What are some of the lessons you can learn when you compare Pilate and Saul?
* Has the Lord ever warned you in a dream or vision?
* Both Pilate and Saul were given prophetic words. Why do you think they chose to turn away from them?
* What do you think is the most prevailing voice in your life? In our culture?
* How can you labor so that God's voice would take its dominion over demonic influence?

Apprehending the truth

As we conclude this chapter I ask myself, "What is the predominant voice in our culture?" I would have to say that it is mass media. The average household in America spends over seven hours a day in front of the television. In addition, social media has captured the time and attention of a generation. Video gaming dominates as a billion dollar industry, stealing the time of millions. Can you imagine if we spent seven hours a day in God's presence, seven hours a day in His Word?

Our lives would take on a different shape altogether! Can you picture a generation that yearns to listen to the Word more than it listens to sitcoms? I believe there is a prophetic culture arising -- the Holy Spirit is moving upon the hearts and minds of millions across the earth. Just as the preeminence of God prevailed throughout the book of Acts, so Jesus will do it once again. Abandonment to the voice of God is possible, even if the noise of our culture is at a deafening tone. Apostles, prophets, evangelists, pastors and teachers are being raised up to fight the powers of darkness. They've been seasoned in the closet of prayer and the Lord is rewarding them.

For more information and products by John,
please visit www.johnharke.com

Printed in the United States
By Bookmasters